THE MAGIC BAKERY

A WMG WRITER'S GUIDE

DEAN WESLEY SMITH

WMG
PUBLISHING

The Magic Bakery
Copyright © 2017 by Dean Wesley Smith
Published by WMG Publishing
Cover and layout copyright © 2017 by WMG Publishing
Cover design by Allyson Longueira/WMG Publishing
Cover art copyright @ vika_nikon/Depositphotos

ISBN-13: 978-1-56146-825-6
ISBN-10: 1-56146-825-8

First published in slightly different form on Dean Wesley Smith's blog at
www.deanwesleysmith.com in 2017

CONTENTS

ALSO BY DEAN WESLEY SMITH

Heinlein's Rules: Five Simple Business Rules for Writing

Stages of a Fiction Writer: Know Where You Stand on the Path to Writing

Writing into the Dark: How to Write a Novel Without an Outline

Killing the Top Ten Sacred Cows of Publishing

Killing the Top Ten Sacred Cows of Indie Publishing

How to Write a Novel in Ten Days

Writing a Novel in Seven Days: A Hands-On Example

Writing a Novel in Five Days While Traveling

INTRODUCTION

Indie writers make great money these days with their small and medium-sized businesses. Some make millions, while at the same time others sell few books.

The writers selling few copies tend to look for reasons why they are not selling. I could spend a lot of time listing all the reasons writers find for a book not selling, but almost always the reason is a very simple business reason.

Inventory.

And a complete failure to understand what they are selling.

But that seemingly simple answer has a vast universe of issues around it. And understanding inventory in publishing takes an understanding of copyright.

So for this book, I am going to extend the metaphor of a Magic Bakery far past its breaking point. Over the years, as I have used this metaphor to help people understand how the business of publishing works, the metaphor seems to help.

And it helps writers understand copyright, the very thing that generates the sales and the money for the business.

So here goes.

Let's open the door to the Magic Bakery, let the wonderful smells of baking bread and fresh doughnuts flow around us. Ignore the racks of cookies sitting in one case and the counter full of wonderful cakes with chocolate frostings.

Head right for the vast cases in the center of the bakery full of pies of all types. All cut and ready to be served either whole or by the slice.

Welcome to your writing business.

The Back Room

Back behind the main counter, beyond that swinging door, is where the magic really occurs.

Flower and flavoring and fresh fruit. Then add sugar and other ingredients and it all comes together in a certain way to create a pie.

A magic pie.

Skill is involved to make the pie, to have it look right, smell right, and most importantly, taste right to the customer.

Years of practiced skill.

Yup, I'm talking about your creation of story. Novel or short story, doesn't matter.

Just like a pie, you take things from the world and combine them in your own unique way to create a wonderful product, a story, for your customers.

Some stories are similar to one another as in a series. Others are as different as a chocolate cream pie would be to a Dutch apple pie. But the customers don't much care.

Sure, each customer has a favorite. Some like the chocolate

cream, others go for cherry. But if you have a regular, a true fan, they will try most everything eventually.

A Few Things This Book Will Cover

So in this book, as each chapter goes on, I will talk about opening your bakery when you are still learning how to bake. (Yes, you should, to answer that basic question right off.)

You are learning how to make your pies look like a pie and have a unique taste that customers will return for over and over. That takes time and work. Learning any skill does.

Also, this book will deal some with how the presentation to the customers in your bakery is critical as well.

And how to even get your customers to the front door of your bakery and then what do you do when they walk through the door to help the customer stay, buy, and return later.

All critical aspects to any business.

Real bakeries or magic. Hardware stores or bookstores.

All businesses worry about those exact problems.

But mostly this book will talk about the magic in the pie itself.

You see, just one element of your magic pie is that when you remove a piece, if you do it correctly, that piece can make you money with a customer and yet the pie will remain whole.

The piece of pie that just made you money magically is back in the pie and ready to sell again.

A magic pie.

And that is only one small aspect of the magic.

So stay with me for some chapters here as I extend this metaphor to the extreme in order to help you understand the value, the importance, and the magic of copyright in your writing.

And also help you understand some real reasons why your work isn't selling many copies in this new, crowded world.

You might not like the reasons. But at least you will know how to fix the problems.

And by the end of this book you will know how to have a bakery where lines of customers form out the door to buy your wonderful work.

That is what this book is all about.

Onward.

1

Digging down into all the vast areas of how writers sell books and the business of selling fiction, I figured the best way to start this would be on the surface, explaining some real logical, but forgotten (by writers), business concepts.

So an example: A young writer (not in age, but in experience) writes and finishes a first novel. And somehow manages to avoid all the traps of rewriting and letting a peer workshop kill the book. Fantastic!

This is a real event and once published should be celebrated. First novels are important to every writer. Get copies out to family, tell friends where the book can be bought, and then go back to writing the next book.

But sadly, the book sells almost no copies. A few to family and friends and nothing else. No one is reading it. And this is the problem of the new world of indie publishing.

Discouragement for no logical reason. You wrote a book your first readers like, why isn't it selling? And pretty soon the young writer is so discouraged they quit.

Now there are lots of reasons that first novel might not be selling, actually. But the main one concerns the Magic Bakery. And basic business.

SOME HISTORY FIRST

In the old days of traditional publishing only, over ten years ago now as I write this, there was only one path into publishing a book and getting it to readers to buy.

The path was simple: You somehow, through some form, got the book to an editor. This took time and often lots of rejections. Years and years of time.

So the advice back then was to mail the book to someone (editor, agent, subway rat who knew someone who could buy the book for a publisher) and then go back to writing the next book.

This process often took so long and was filled with so many rejections, a writer either quit (most) or kept writing and got better. My first sold novel was my third written novel. And my fourth written novel never saw the light of day.

The time it took allowed writers with drive to improve skills and keep writing. The system forced it.

NOW THE NEW WORLD

There is no system. No one forces a writer to wait to get a book out to readers and no writer should wait. That old system of gatekeepers was too stupid for words.

But now the young writer puts the book out there and there are no sales.

What could be wrong? Why doesn't the book sell?

Clearing out some basic reasons first...

... Your cover sucks and looks like a beginner did it or the art.

... Your sales blurb is so long, so full of plot, and so passive it puts readers to sleep.

... Your opening is so thin, so full of action with no depth, no one would buy it.

... You don't know genre and put the book on the wrong shelf in the electronic stores.

But sure, you might have those things wrong, you fix them, and your book still won't sell.

Why not?

The Magic Bakery is why not.

A PERSONAL STORY FIRST

In early 1977 I decided I wanted to start a used bookstore while I was going to college for a degree in architecture. And not an antiquarian bookstore, but a type of bookstore I had seen starting up in California when I was a golf professional. Basically a paperback exchange.

This was a fairly new concept in 1977 and it sounded like fun. But I had one major issue. I had maybe 400 books I wanted to part with in my collection. So the idea was sort of just a pipe dream until one day I was going up the escalator into my bank when I saw a small For Rent sign on a big metal door at the top of five stairs at the top of the escalator.

You turned right to go into the bank, the stairs went up to the left and to this big metal fire door. I went through the big door into a small lobby. An attorney had a large office ahead, a doctor to the left, and down a dark hallway was the For Rent sign.

An office smaller than most kid's bedrooms. $75 per month. I was hooked.

My wife-at-the-time wanted nothing to do with the idea of starting a business. She was working on her masters. So I promised her I would keep the spending under $200 to start it. I rented the place for $100 for a month counting the deposit, bought about $50 in old pine lumber and built shelves to fill the place. Every wall and in the middle of the small room as well. I bought a used desk for $10 and then took up my 400 books. They looked really, really sad.

Almost the entire store was empty. Pathetic didn't begin to describe it.

So I told my wife-at-the-time I needed to go buy some books and headed out that weekend to find books around the Pacific Northwest. I managed to bring home another thousand paperbacks.

I spent more than $200, but not part of our household funds. I had been playing on blackjack teams in Vegas for a number of years before I met my-then-wife and never told her I had money in cutout paperbacks in my book collections that I had been using to pay for college. The rule about my books was that if they were in a bag, no one touched them. No one bothered to ask me how I could get through college without a loan and only worked a few nights tending bar and driving a school bus. Her parents paid for her expenses.

(I finally told her a few years ago. She is still a friend.)

So I took three hundred out of my own "college fund" and bought the books. They still looked very sad in the room full of empty shelves.

I hung out a sign. No one came at first. Nothing to come for.

So I kept searching for more books, garage sales, you name

it, and slowly people started to find the little store down the hall. And I had enough books by that point to sell them or trade them something.

Eventually I grew out of that room, took over the big lawyer's office and then a year later moved the store into its own building down on the street. All while finishing my masters in architecture and then starting law school.

Magic Bakery

The young writer has their one finished book. It is up for sale and no one is buying. Covers, blurbs, opening, and self problem fixed.

No one is buying the book.

Why not?

Imagine you are a customer and you see this great sign for a bakery. Makes your mouth water at the idea of getting something.

You go in. The bell on the door jingles and around you are massive empty shelves and display cases.

All empty except for up near the cash register is this one pie.

If you were the customer, what would you do? Be honest...

You would turn around and walk out, of course. No way are you going to buy from a bakery that only has one product sitting there all alone.

There is no magic to this concept. It is just a logical customer reaction.

You have no product yet.

But that can be fixed...

Now if you stay writing, creating, you will slowly fill the shelves and display cases.

And since in the Magic Bakery nothing spoils, eventually the shelves and the cases will be full. And as you do get more product, some people will stay and buy.

I have over 300 different products in my magic bakery. And many of the products are in different forms.

You know the business concept at play: Selection and flavors. Things to bring the customers to the register to buy.

This concept is not so magic. It is just logical business.

So if you are discouraged about your first or third novel not selling what you hoped, just think of that big empty bakery and go back to writing. Given enough time, you will fill it.

Or at least get enough product in the bakery so that people will start buying as they did in my little bookstore.

2

So what makes this bakery so magic anyway? Copyright, that's what.

As the *Copyright Handbook* says, "Copyright is the legal device that provides the creator of a work of art or literature, or a work that conveys information or idea, the right to control how the work is used."

So what is so magic about that? All countries in the world have copyright protections in one form or another. As of the writing of this chapter, almost all countries in the world have signed onto one copyright convention or another, agreeing to the basic aspects of copyright protections.

In fact, here in the States, copyright protection was written into the Constitution right from the beginning, it is that important.

But what makes it magic? Actually just one phrase in that definition I gave you is the source of the magic.

"... the right to control how the work is used."

SPOILED COPYRIGHT

Spoiled copyright is a concept that is flat hard to imagine now in this modern world of electronic shelves. As I said in the last chapter, that pie you have sitting there in your shop will never spoil.

Copyright never spoils.

And since we are using a pie as a metaphor for copyright, imagine baking a pie and it will taste just as good five years later as it did on the day you baked it.

Or 70 years later. Or 100 years later if you live for another 30 years after the baking.

This idea that copyright never spoils is almost impossible for writers coming out of traditional publishing to wrap minds around. It took me some time I must admit.

Traditional publishing companies (for decades) used the produce model for books. They treated books like fruit. Not kidding.

The publishers would set a time the book would appear. Then the book would appear and within a set time the book would "spoil" in the eyes of the publisher and bookstores and be pulled and returned to the publisher for credit. For all intents and purposes, that book was dead.

Rotten fruit. Very few books survived that fate. Very, very few.

The reality was that the copyright was just fine. It actually hadn't spoiled. Just the publishers thought of it as dead.

And so did the authors.

And even if an author got the rights back from the company, chances are the book never saw the light of day again.

Writers who got books reverted still had the right to

control the use of the book, sure, but the belief was that the copyright had spoiled and the book or story was done. Used up. Rotted fruit.

Then along comes this new world and electronic shelves with unlimited space. And suddenly all those dead and spoiled books took on a new life.

The magic of copyright never spoiling.

A book that only had four weeks on the shelf 20 years ago now had a chance to find a new audience who weren't even born the first time the book appeared.

My first novel came out in 1989. So basically anyone under 35 would not have read that book unless they found it in a used bookstore. Now that first novel is back out and earning me money for the first time in almost 30 years. And finding new readers who might enjoy it.

It is in this new world that the hard fact of a copyright never spoiling actually started to become a reality to many writers.

It also, after about six or seven years, started to dawn on the major publishers as well, which is why they now buy all rights for the entire life of a copyright. They now understand as well that copyright has value over long periods of time and won't spoil. (They haven't figured out what to do with the rights they are keeping, but they have figured out enough to keep them.)

The magic in the copyright-filled pie now rules. But like with any good magic, you have to know how to unleash the spell. I will get to that.

FIRST SALE AND ELECTRONIC LICENSE

Right now, before I go any farther here in chapter two,

I had better get everyone on the same page with a few more basics.

Copyright is the protection of the expression. So when you sell a paper copy of the book, you transfer no copyright. Copyright can only be transferred by a written agreement. You are basically selling a block of paper. Nothing more.

That physical book, that pile of paper, exists and the new owner of the book can sell the block of paper itself. But they have no right to take any of the words from the book and use them.

None. They bought the paper, not the words on the paper.

This is called the First Sale Doctrine and it applies mostly only to paper books.

So in Magic Bakery terms, when a customer in the Magic Bakery buys a piece of your pie (paperback piece), the piece remains in the pie even though the customer gets to enjoy the taste of the pie and walk out of the store with a pile of paper. The piece never leaves the pie.

Magic. An ever-replenishing inventory. Wish I would have had that with my bookstore.

Now we have the new electronic books. So you have the slice of your pie called "Electronic Rights" up on Amazon.

Basically what you have done is rented from the big Amazon Mall some space to include your Magic Bakery inside their mall.

You also have your Magic Bakery in the Kobo Mall, the B&N Mall, and so on.

When a customer comes through your door and wants a piece of pie in electronic form, they can enjoy it, but they have bought nothing. They have licensed the right to read it only.

Nothing more.

They cannot trade or sell that electronic copy. They own

nothing and in fact, you never sold them anything, you licensed to the reader the right to read the work.

Nothing more. **First Sales does not apply to electronic copies.**

So either selling paper copies to a reader or licensing electronic copy to a reader, your pie remains whole sitting in your Magic Bakery.

So over a month's time you sell or license 100 pieces of that pie. The pie has not changed or diminished or spoiled in any fashion.

Every store on the planet wishes for magic inventory like that. Only writers and artists and other copyright holders have it.

WHY ONLY A PIECE?

This is now where the real fun and magic starts to happen.

Why didn't I say that a person buying the paper book didn't buy the entire pie?

Because the entire pie is not just paperback rights. Or electronic licensing rights. Or audio rights.

Say you write a novel. The novel is the pie. The copyright is what you license from the pie, the pieces of the pie, basically.

Each area of the pie is a different right. One small slice is paperback rights, one small slice is hardback rights, one small slice is electronic, one small slice is audio, and on and on.

You never sell the entire pie.

Now going to traditional publishers, they want to buy the entire pie and put your magic in their store. And writers are doing that all the time, allowing their magic pie to leave their bakery.

Visualize it this way: Some person from New York publishing in a suit walks into your Magic Bakery and flops some small amount of money on the counter. You say sure and they take your magic pie and turn and leave your store, leaving that spot on the counter forever empty. FOREVER EMPTY. They walk your magic pie down the mall to their massive anchor store and put your pie in their Magic Bakery.

You have now sold inventory to a store that is competing with your store.

And you will never get that pie back.

In real world terms, this is "all rights for the life of the copyright" contracts. If you see that in your contract for anything, RUN!!

In coming chapters will be a ton more about this problem. And a lot more about how you can divide up the pie, make more money from each slice, and never lose control.

And remember, every story you finish, every novel, every article (including this Magic Bakery book I am writing right now here in front of you) is a new pie. Another product to have in my display cases and on my shelves when a customer comes through the door of my Magic Bakery.

And the larger the store you have, the more product you have, the more customers and the more money you make if you keep the floors swept, the glass on the display cases clean, and a smile on your face.

Frighteningly enough, it really does work that way.

3

How do you slice a magic pie? The answer is simply as many ways as you want.

The wonderful thing about copyright is that you can license any part of it. And you can name the part and dictate the terms and define the shape of the part.

I know this is difficult to imagine. And the pie analogy sort of falls apart because pie is a physical thing that can only be sliced in so many ways.

But image the pie is solid and you have a saw that can slice off a piece so thin you can barely see the slice under a microscope.

Yup, you can do that with a magic pie.

Honest.

A few broad examples...

Say you were approached by a publisher in a small country you had to go to Google to find on the map. The publisher wanted to translate and print your book only in that country's language. And only in hardback with dust jacket. And only five hundred copies. And only for one year.

You figure out where the country is at and say sure. The contract comes and you get your saw and slice off a tiny, tiny thin license. Translation rights into (country's language only) for hardback only for a run of 500 copies only for only a year.

In a year that tiny, tiny slice will reappear back in the magic pie of copyright for that novel and you can sell it again.

Or say you have a novel headed into a game or movie. You have retained all toy rights. So a manufacture of resin busts comes to you and wants to license the right to make busts of your characters in a limited edition run of one thousand copies signed by the artist.

Out comes the saw and you slice off a tiny, tiny thin license for resin character busts for a limited one thousand copies. And you sell the plush license to the characters to another company and the action figures of the characters to another company and so on and so on.

All limited-time licenses because you understand copyright and contracts.

My wife, Kristine Kathryn Rusch, on her blog, did most of a year about publishing contracts and there is now a book out of those blogs. That is all basic stuff, but you have to know the basics before you can learn how to use the saw to cut tiny, tiny thin pieces.

And you cannot do that if you have allowed the magic pie to leave your control, your Magic Bakery.

Some Horror Stories from the Magic Bakery

These are about magic pies leaving your bakery.

First off, agents, especially book and Hollywood agents, are not your friends, folks. Avoid at all costs. All horror stories start and end with the word "agent."

I am not kidding.

Here is a real-life Magic Bakery horror story. Agent sold a writer's novel series to Hollywood. The writer was uninformed about how copyright really worked and the agent was either a crook or stupid or didn't realize what he was doing. Take your pick.

The contract the writer signed sold (not licensed) the Hollywood studio rights to the books in the series. What the writer didn't know about what his agent told him to sign was that it also gave away all control of his characters.

And Hollywood didn't want him writing any more of those characters since they controlled them. Writer lost in the court. He signed the contract.

In other words, what the writer did was stand behind the counter of his Magic Bakery and watch the Hollywood agent carry his magic pie out of the door and take it to another store to make money for someone else.

Another real story.

Remember a writer by the name of Clancy? Wrote this novel called *The Hunt for Red October* that became a major bestseller and a movie. It had a character in it called Jack Ryan.

Clancy stood behind his counter and watched the magic pie leave his bakery for $500 total. Someone else sliced up the pie as they wanted and the pie became a bestselling book and then a movie. Eventually Clancy sued for the right to even use Jack Ryan as a character again in another book.

They settled and he had to pay to use his own character.

Why? Because he let the magic pie that was *The Hunt for Red October* leave his store to make someone else money.

I bet I could come up with another 20 of these horror stories just off the top of my head. After 40 years in this business I have heard so many of them it makes me sick.

Staying with the Analogy

You have a recipe for a wonderful magic pie. You go to all the work to create that pie and use special ingredients that make that pie special.

Then not only do you sell the magic pie you created and let it leave your business, you sell the recipe to the pie as well and all the ingredients. And you sell the right to ever make anything similar to it again.

Why would anyone do that?

I ask myself that every day because it happens 100s, if not 1,000s of times every day in Magic Bakeries all over the world.

Writers do not know what they have, do not understand the value of the golden goose that is the story or novel they created.

So they sell their magic pie for all rights for the life of the copyright to a major publisher. Movie rights, toy rights, translation rights, video, audio, electronic, paper, and on and on. All making someone else money.

And even worse, the writers often sign a contract saying they will not go back and make more magic pies without permission from the buyer of the last magic pie.

Might as well shut that Magic Bakery down. It is finished.

Go to any convention and watch the young writers flocking to agents, listen to the discussions about how to break into traditional publishing.

Then as you listen, realize what they are working so hard to do is make sure their magic pie leaves their Magic Bakery.

Summary Statement

Never ever let your entire magic pie out of your control. License slices only and then for a limited time only. Nothing more.

And slice the pieces you do license very, very thin. As thin as you can.

And then keep making new magic pies to fill the shelves.

4

I started off chapter three with a question and an answer: "How do you slice a magic pie? The answer is simply as many ways as you want."

But first you have to have a magic pie to slice.

You have to have copyright to license. And that is the rub, the place where so many writers flat run into a massive wall. It takes time and a lot of practice and knocking down personal demons to produce new stories and novels regularly.

Anyone can do it for a short time. A year. Maybe two. But then with just a few cases in their Magic Bakery half full and the rest of the bakery still empty, the writer fades away.

The magic pies don't spoil as I talked about earlier, but they sure gather dust. No one comes through the door and no one keeps up the bakery.

When the writer stops caring about their own business, the business dies. It is called quitting and it is the only way to fail in this modern world of publishing.

Now I understand how hard this is. Clearly understand.

And this problem of looking at empty shelves almost got me as well.

So a personal story...

As Kris and I moved from traditional publishing to indie publishing, I got the statement from young writers over and over how easy I had it because I already had work.

Well, I knew how to tell stories, sure. And I had sold millions of books and had made my living in publishing since 1988. Sure.

But the indie world made me into a flat beginner. So when some young writer with three or four or five novels said that I had this huge advantage over them, I just nodded and said nothing.

The only real advantage I had was that I was a better storyteller.

You see, the dirty truth was I had no books. Well, I actually had two, one was my first published novel I had the rights back to and one was a thriller I had written and then tossed in a drawer. And I had a ton of short stories.

For almost all of my career, I was a media writer and a ghost writer. I wrote over one hundred novels under pen names or media books and I didn't own a one of them. I had baked the magic pie in someone else's bakery.

So I had nothing but the short stories and I didn't feel I wanted to bring the thriller or the first novel out right off the bat.

I felt I needed to fill my Magic Bakery.

It felt impossible, I must admit.

I would stand in that Magic Bakery and stare at all the empty shelves and wonder how in the world at my age I would ever fill them. In other words, I had to start my writing career completely over in my 60s.

So with two novel pies sitting in the back room and my bakery almost completely empty except for some shelves of short story pies to one side, I started to work in 2011. All of the shelves were cleaned and polished and just waiting for me to fill them.

Waiting for me to get baking.

I did some more short stories to get started and then lost most of a year to a personal friend's death and estate.

By the time I got back to writing, it was almost 2013. And again I did more short stories to try to get going.

Then in the summer of 2013 I decided I really needed to get baking. I was tired of staring at all the empty shelves.

So I started up *Smith's Monthly,* which needed a novel, four short stories, and a serial every month. And I had to write it all. Every word of a monthly seventy thousand word magazine.

I wrote like crazy that summer to get a few novel pies on the shelf and the first issue came out in October 2013. I am a little behind at the moment here in 2017 as I write this, but I expect to be caught up by October 2017 with the 4th full year without missing a month. And then I plan to start into the fifth year.

Imagine in October a wall of my Magic Bakery will be full of forty-eight magic pies with the sign over the wall *Smith's Monthly* pies.

After four years I now have pies of different sorts filling my bakery.

These nonfiction books taken from blog posts.

The short stories have all been published standalone and a slice of each novel was taken and licensed to WMG to publish standalone.

And I combined slices of the short stories to be in collections and so on. Not counting short stories, last year alone I did twenty-six major books. The year before over thirty. This year will again be over thirty.

I went from having a mostly empty bakery to a decent inventory in my Magic Bakery in four years.

Over a hundred major products and hundreds of short stories.

And the customers are coming, even though I have done very little, if any advertising.

Seems people like the taste of a Cold Poker Gang pie or a Seeders Universe pie or a Poker Boy pie.

This Takes Time

There are a number of hot, young (in numbers of books) gurus out there at this moment preaching how to sell more books by this or that advertising device. Some of the advice is pretty good. And WMG is following some of it in moderation.

But almost without fail, these "experts" have an almost empty Magic Bakery. They have gotten very, very good at driving customers into their empty store, but have forgotten the reason to have the store in the first place.

Think folks. You might, through some advertising hype or another, go into a store you have never visited. We all do. Standard business stuff. But if you walked into the store with only a few things on the shelves, would you make it a point of going back?

Nope.

In our north Pop Culture Collectables store, we have over 20,000 books and 100,000 comics, toys, cars, games, and collectables of all sorts. It fills four large rooms and when someone comes in they are always surprised at how much we have and they always take time to explore all four rooms.

And they often buy something they didn't even know they wanted.

If they came through the door and we had two collectable cars, an old toy, five used paperbacks, and six used comics in the four rooms, think anyone would bother to stay? Or come back?

Nope.

It has taken us over a year now to get the store as full as it is. And we had all the inventory in the warehouse. It took a year to get it all out and priced.

Things take time.

As writers, we must create our own inventory. And that flat takes time.

But it will never happen if you don't start.

And it will never happen if you quit.

How to Even Start?

First—As I suggest in a number of classes, do an inventory of your Magic Bakery.

Everything. Every article that might be combined into a book, every short story, every novel.

Everything that you own copyright on and have created. Even stuff still in the back room you are too afraid to bring out and put on a shelf.

Second—See if there is any way to create new products with that inventory? You know, take a small slice from five short stories and combine it into a collection. Things like that.

Or get your work up on BundleRabbit so people can ask for the bundling slice of your pies. And so on and so on.

Third—Figure out your hours. How much time do you spend writing each week creating new product? What is stopping you from getting some of the work in the back room out to the shelves?

In other words, find your demons. Check Heinlein's Five Rules and be honest about which rule you are falling down on.

Fourth—Make a five-year and ten-year plan. Expect it to take time to fill your shelves of your Magic Bakery.

Early on, make your focus not on getting customers through the door to be disappointed, but on making your Magic Bakery a place where people will want to return over and over when they do find it.

When you start thinking of your writing as a business and a retail store, it really is amazing how clear some basics about writing become.

I knew this four plus years ago when I started filling my shelves. And I do not plan on slowing down because my bakery really is magic. I have as much room as I need to expand when my inventory starts filling the shelves.

And I plan on doing a lot of expanding over the next 10 years.

5

I get a lot of questions about pen names and if writers should use pen names in this modern world of publishing.

So let me use the Magic Bakery to explain my answer to that question.

Now understand, the reason for this book about the Magic Bakery is to help writers understand copyright and the magic power of copyright in this world.

But the metaphor of the bakery can help in business logic as well.

And in sales.

And in promotions. For example, understanding the power of free is clearly illustrated in the Magic Bakery and I will get to that in a later chapter.

But for this chapter, I want to focus on Pen Names.

The New World

In the old world, we had to go down the mall and open up

brand new stores and try to fill them every time we started a new pen name.

One store for every pen name.

So most of the time the pen name stores just looked empty and the readers, even if they liked something, had little else to buy.

In this new world, you keep all books under one name.

Think about it. When a customer walks into one of our Pop Culture Collectable stores here on the coast, they see toys, antique jewelry, games, comics, books, cookie jars, clocks, cars, and a bunch more.

We have all the sections in different parts of the store.

So you have a Magic Bakery. A customer walks through the door.

To the right, filling a wall, are all the science fiction pies and cakes. Straight ahead are the romance cakes and rolls, to the left, the mystery pies and snacks.

Then off to one side is the young adult section.

And on all the displays in the middle of the floor are all the short story pies, cakes, rolls, and such.

All are clearly marked so there is no confusion, the descriptions on each shelf clear as to the flavors of the pies.

The customer doesn't have to go to five half-empty stores to find all of your work. They found it all in one store, under one name.

Being Clear

There is no reason at all in this new world of reader-controlled publishing to use a pen name. Keep everything under one name and display that name in bright letters on the outside of your store.

Brand your store to that one name so readers can find everything you do.

They may not like the taste of your mystery blood pies, but they love your romance sweet pies.

Let the readers decide. Give them something to shop for.

Sure, with our stories, we could open a comic store, a toy car store, a collectible card store, a clock store, an antique toy store. Sure.

But it was easier to keep it all in one large store and put it all under one name.

Do the same with your writing.

One name, one Magic Bakery.

6

I get questions all the time about free. Should an author put up their book for free? How about their first book in a series? Does leaving something up for free forever work?

Interestingly enough, The Magic Bakery works perfectly to illustrate the answer to these questions so writers can decide for themselves.

All I'm going to be talking about in this chapter is basic, standard-retail sales practices. I won't tell you one thing new in the world. You can see some of these practices working every day from grocery stores to music stores.

But explaining these practices to authors who do not understand basic sales of retail has been an issue. And thus extreme myths have built up around the use of free in book sales.

And it seems everyone has an opinion, often not based on anything but "It worked for me for a little bit."

So using the Magic Bakery, let me show you some of the

simple ways that free can be an effective sales tool for your products.

And some of the really boneheaded ways to use free that will hurt your business.

Copyright in Free

One quick point here in this book focused on mostly understanding copyright. When you give a story or book away for free, you do not lose the copyright protection on that work in any way.

My Basic Rule of Thumb About Free

Nothing ever sits on a bookstore shelf, real-wood shelf or electronic shelf, for free.

It is a very simple rule and when I say that to someone they automatically think I am against free. I am not. I am against using free in a poor business way. I use free all the time to help sales, as does WMG Publishing.

So now to the Magic Bakery to illustrate why this rule works for me and for others.

First, a simple positive way to use free.

A customer comes into your bakery. You have a wall of about 20 pies that are your novels, some are grouped together because they are series pies. All are priced. You may have a reduced price on a few first pies, but all are priced in a reasonable and fair manner.

You have a large counter in the middle of the room of short story pies, smaller and at a lower price than the larger pies on the wall.

You have specials you are running around the cash register.

And there, beside the specials, near the cash register, on top of a glass counter, you have a plate of bite-sized pieces of your latest creation for readers to sample.

The sign under that plate says, "Take one."

You have maybe a dozen pieces on the plate with small plastic forks and when those pieces of pie are gone, you take the plate to the back to wash. The idea is to get customers, for free, sampling your work so they will buy.

This form of use of free is standard in almost every form of store. You see this a lot in grocery stores. And in bakeries.

For authors, we do this as sample chapters in the back of another book.

Or free short stories for a week on a web site. And so on. Lots of ways to give limited, small samples in this modern world.

The key in sales are LIMITED and SHORT TERM.

Keep free short term and limited and never put it on a bookshelf anywhere.

Now the wrong way to use free.

A customer walks through your door and you have a wall of 20 pies in glass cases, all the smaller short story pies in a case in the center, and some specials near the cash register.

And there on your wall are three pies that say, "Free."

And a bunch of short stories that are "Free."

The customer can take an entire pie for free or buy one. As a customer, what would you do? Duh. You take the free pie and leave.

(Or you question the value of any of the pies and leave without anything.)

And, because of copyright, the pie is still sitting there after someone takes it for free. Magic Bakery, remember? So more and more people start hearing you are giving away free pies in your Magic Bakery.

And pretty soon your customers start to change. The only people who come through the door are people who only want the free stuff. They would never buy something under any circumstances, but you are giving your pies away for free, so they take one.

Pretty soon there would be lines out the door to get your free pies and you would make nothing. The free takers would crowd out and devalue the pies you are trying to sell.

That is the wrong use of free for any reason you may want to make up to justify it.

Now discounting is another topic. There are ways to discount first books in a series to entice buyers into getting into a series. This is also a common practice in most stores, actually.

A Personal Example

I live in a small town that has a huge discount mall. Now all smart shoppers know that the big chains mark up the prices before lowering them for the discount stores. Makes the "discount" price look better to those looking for deals.

Now I use the mall as a place to walk on rainy days. And at times, I go into stores to look around. The stores have their "discount" racks clear to the back. The discount racks are what is left of the normal merchandise that hasn't sold and they are just trying to clear.

But to get to that actually discounted stuff, I have to walk through their entire store. And every-so-often, that sales trick gets me and I see something I don't mind paying full price for.

That is a standard retail trick of discounting to get a customer in to buy other stuff.

But not one place in any of those stores is there a free item. Why not? Because they are all businesses, that's why not.

Writers need to learn how to act and think like regular business people.

So How to Use Free in Your Bakery?

A one-day give-away of one of your pies. Only for a very limited time and only for a very limited number.

I try not to laugh in writer's faces who tell me they have "sold" 20,000 books and when I ask, they actually gave away that many books.

Free is not a sale.

Free is free. A sale is when you make something from the exchange. So follow basic retail practices. If you are going to give something away for free, do it for a short time and a limited number.

And then make it special.

And again, never put it on a shelf of any bookstore.

Once again, over the years, I have tried not to laugh when writers go on about how to game Amazon's system and get their book there for free. I have laughed many times, but not in the writer's faces, luckily.

You ever wonder why you have to game the smartest business on the planet at the moment to get something on their shelves for free? Oh, let me think— They don't make any money.

Yet they are a business. You are taking up their shelf space with something that makes them no money.

You walk into our Pop Culture Collectable stores here in

town and there isn't one thing on the shelves for free. So do we give things away at times? Sure. Free comic book day once a year. Things like that. Promotions that are limited and short term to bring customers into the store to buy other things.

Limited and short term.

There is no reason at all for us to go to the time and energy to get inventory and then put it on our shelves for free. No reason for any business to do that.

And certainly no reason for you to do that in your Magic Bakery.

Just imagine walking into a pie shop and there is a wall of pies that all look great, and five or six of them say, "Free" under it. Try to imagine that.

If you can't imagine that, good. But if you want to start learning how to use free correctly, then start looking around at other businesses outside of electronic books and see what they do with free.

In the business and sales world, free is a powerful, powerful tool if used correctly and for the right reasons.

Make sure your Magic Bakery is a place someone can come to buy your wonderful work. And that free is used in ways (not on the shelves of your bakery) to entice buyers into your bakery.

Free is short time, limited supply, and never on the major bookstore shelves.

Simple Magic Bakery rules-of-thumb that are nothing more than standard retail business practices.

7

I knew I was going to need to talk about this topic in a chapter and honestly, have dreaded it. Writers, especially newer writers have no understanding of the value of their own work and how others value it.

So with that problem in mind, I am going to try to add a level of understanding of value of copyright to this book. For most of you, I will fail at this, but at least I can say I tried right here in Chapter Seven.

I'm calling this chapter "Perceived Value" of the inventory in the Magic Bakery.

I cannot even begin to count the hundreds and hundreds of times I have heard a new writer say, "I'm new so I should give my stuff away or sell it for only 99 cents."

I will not get into a pricing discussion here. There are lots of other places out there in the vast world of the inner-tubes to shout about your price being better or worse than another price. Go to it.

I am talking about "Perceived Value."

The Dollar Store

Here in the US, there are numbers of chains of stores known for selling things at one dollar. To make sure I was correct in my perceived value of the goods in the Dollar Store, I stopped by the one here on the coast a few days ago.

Lots of small toys, all cheap. Lots of household stuff you could get for a buck in any supermarket.

Everything that was either normally a buck in another store or some cheap knockoff. The entire store.

Now, if I had gone in there looking for a fine bottle of wine, I would have been very disappointed. But I went in there knowing I would be finding exactly what I found. Cheap stuff worth less than a buck.

My "Perceived Value" of that store was right on. I went in expecting cheap and I got cheap. Both in price and quality of the goods.

Let me repeat that: **I got cheap price and a cheap quality of the goods.**

And I was not surprised.

So I log onto a website for a writer I do not know. (Most writers, both experienced and new. I have no way of knowing the difference. And neither do readers.) And I see nothing but free and 99 cent books. What do I expect?

I expect a cheap and lower level of goods.

And since I like to be entertained and only have so much reading time, I will go find another author. Yes, I will pay more. But my two hours of reading won't be wasted.

Quality wine vs. a buck bottle of whine. Sorry, I like a good wine.

Readers are no different. (Sure, there are the only buy

cheap or free reader and they sometimes find something worth reading. I got that. Not my customer.)

The Discount Mall Principle

Perceived value is a major art form in discount malls. We have a massive discount mall here and all of the stores in that mall show the original price on every item and then the discount price and the sale price and then for today only take off another 25% if you can stand on one leg and snort.

But that original price is right there on the tag. You can get a $200 coat for today only if you snort loud enough for $49.99. The customer has a perceived value of the coat at $200. Wow, what a deal and they grab it.

Also top brand-name stores are in the mall. Nike for example. Just by walking in that door the customer knows of the perceived value of a Nike shoe.

The Magic Bakery Value

Since you own your Magic Bakery and create all the product, you have the freedom to set your own prices. A logical way to do that is to figure out what other books in your genre are selling for. Then look at what Amazon suggests is a sweet spot.

In other words, toss out all your emotions about the lack of value of your work and do the research to figure out what is a good price range for your genre.

It really is very simple. And then, if you have the price stated clearly, you can do those special one-day sales to see how well your customers can snort.

You set the perceived value of your work.

Do not set it with emotions and fear and self-loathing.

37

Pretty sure self-loathing is not a principle in business pricing economics. (Except for young writers in fiction. Since new writers gained this control, they have taken self-loathing of their own work into the gutter of pricing. Stop now. Just stop.)

The New Traditional Model of Perceived Value

Here is where things get tough and I will not turn one person's head, but I have to talk about it.

Intellectual property (IP) is what makes up all the pies and cakes in your bakery. Everyone got that?

IP has a value. (Yeah, Dean, we know, we know.)

But alas, you do not know at what level.

Ever wonder why over the last ten years traditional publishing contracts have gone to all-rights for the life of the copyright?

Ever wonder why it is almost impossible now to get books back from traditional publishers once you have sold all rights?

Because IP has a value. Not just a sales value of possible income earned. An accounting value to major corporations.

There are many, many companies now that are buying IP and have no intent of ever marketing it or publishing it or making it into a movie. They simply want the IP.

Yes, your IP. (Your pie, your cake.)

I'll bet you didn't know that there are a ton of major companies out there with the only job, the only reason they exist, is to value IP for other companies.

Don't believe me? Simply Google "IP Valuation" and then do some reading.

THIS PRACTICE HAS ONLY BEEN AROUND FOR A DECADE OR TWO. Yeah, about the time traditional publishers stopped putting in even decent claw-back clauses for your rights and bought everything.

They bought your entire magic pie and they took it out of your store and they know how to value it. They do not care if anything is ever made. They need the value for their bottom lines in the accounting.

Your pie adds value to the big corporation base.

At the moment there are four or five ways that are basic ways that these valuation companies value your IP. But a couple of the sites said there are over 25 other alternative methods.

Trust me, traditional publishing, after grabbing your IP for next to nothing, leaving your bakery with your pie, know all the tricks of making your IP far, far more valuable to their bottom line than what they actually paid.

There is even one method called "Relief from Royalty" that allows the valuation to be made up in case they needed to sell the movie rights, or the translation rights, or whatever. And assuming all those rights did sell in this made-up "arms-length" scenario, that would be the value of your IP.

And did you know one major thing about IP??? It is a property and thus can, under certain circumstances, be depreciated by the corporation.

So they buy your IP for $5,000 because they promised you a movie. They now own it.

They value it under one of the many ways of valuation far, far higher than what they paid and get some major valuation company to sign off on it.

Then they start depreciating it to get the tax deductions on other money coming in. Only one minor way.

Another method is the "Venture Capital Method" which is a name for what I try to get writers to understand about the value of their copyright over the 70 years past death. This method basically values the possible future cash flow OVER THE ASSETS LIFE. And there is no adjustment to any probability of success. Just a wild guess as to what it might make over its lifetime. Yup.

Your wonderful pie is nothing more than an accounting trick.

(If you want to read one good article about this on the IP Watchdog site, it is here. But do the Google search. It will blow you away.)

Summary

—Never sell all rights. Never let your pie leave your bakery for any reason or any amount of money.

—Research and learn the common indie prices for your books, both paper and electronic. (Ignore traditional publishing prices, as you have just figured out, they sort of don't much care any more.)

—Grow a sense of self-worth that your writing has value. Then treat it as it has value.

How your readers perceive your work is everything in this new world. Start making sure they don't think of your stuff as cheap plastic doomed for the Dollar Store.

8

Doors to the Bakery

Any business must have a way to get into the business.

For example, at our North collectable store here in town you can enter through an interior staircase and climb, or climb an exterior staircase. Both methods take some work for customers and we also have a special entrance in the back that comes in without stairs.

Three entrances. We have the store full of enough cool stuff, we hope it is worth the customer's climb.

So how do readers, publishers, and others get into your bakery to buy your magic pies?

The fun of Magic Bakeries, there are many actual doors.

Far more doors, actually, than you have products in the bakery.

Yeah, a Magic Bakery is a strange place, but it is magical after all.

An example: Say you have written one short story only and published it.

The magic pie that is that short story is sitting on the shelf all by itself. Your bakery is empty and no customers are really going to stop by, even if they happen to find your one story somewhere.

So at that moment in time, your bakery only has a few dozen doors and nothing to hold customers when they arrive.

Why that many doors? Because you have been smart and put the story out wide, meaning Amazon, B&N, Kobo, D2D and so on through all the places D2D and Smashwords distribute to. (I'll talk about paper below.)

So for the sake of simple, say that your one story is for sale at a dozen places.

One story times a dozen places is a dozen ways someone can find your story and thus enter your Magic Bakery.

Every Story is a Door into Your Work

This concept flies in the face of the old myths about writing slow, only doing a book a year or two. Sorry if you are still using one of those myths as an excuse to not sit and write much. You need to figure out how to change that.

Productivity is king in this modern world and the reason is simple. Every story or novel or collection you put out is a doorway to your Magic Bakery and all your other work.

So say I have 300 different products out there in one form or another. (I have more.) Each product is sold wide. So I have about 3,600 doors into my bakery that readers can come through at any moment. Or movie folks or gaming offers or overseas publishers.

Those doors are all over the world, folks.

This is the basic concept of discoverability in this Magic Bakery metaphor.

The more work you have out for sale, the more readers can discover all of your work.

Every Story is a Door into Your Work

This concept flies in the face of the old myths about writing slow, only doing a book a year or two. Sorry if you are still using one of those myths as an excuse to not sit and write much. You need to figure out how to change that.

Productivity is king in this modern world and the reason is simple. Every story or novel or collection you put out is a doorway to your Magic Bakery and all your other work.

So say I have 300 different products out there in one form or another. (I have more.) Each product is sold wide. So I have about 3,600 doors into my bakery that readers can come through at any moment. Or movie folks or gaming offers or overseas publishers.

Those doors are all over the world, folks.

This is the basic concept of discoverability in this Magic Bakery metaphor.

The more work you have out for sale, the more readers can discover all of your work.

Other Doors?

There are hundreds and hundreds of ways to get readers through one of your doors. Again, your Magic Bakery must have product, be clean, and well lit, meaning people can see what flavor of magic pie they want to try.

An example of one great way is to sell a short story to a

magazine or anthology. The door is your story in that book or magazine, which will be different when you publish the story out wide later on.

For example, you sell a story to *Asimov's* and it is printed in their magazine. They get to about a hundred thousand readers through their varied means. That door is now open into your bakery because readers there can enjoy your story and follow your name through the door into your other work.

Bundles are another great door that opens and closes. For example, as I write this, I have novels in two great bundles. Now both novels are out there wide in electronic and paper. But for three weeks, each novel in each bundle will have a new door that readers can follow to my Magic Bakery and all my other work.

There are many, many other ways. From Bookbub to Facebook promotions to Amazon ads to giving a story away on your blog every week and so on. So, so many ways and more being created every day.

But the basic premise is that any time you can set up a way for readers to find one of your stories, it creates a door into your bakery and all your other work.

Create Doors by Creating More Product

One of the most common questions I get is about collections. The question is always in a form like this: "If I have five of my short stories in a collection, should I also publish them stand-alone?"

My answer is always yes, of course. A collection is one door times all the places you have it for sale. For sake of the math, say 1 x 12 equals 12 doors.

If you put up the stories as stand-alone stories as well, you have created 60 more doors. So with stories in a collection and stand-alone, you would have at least 72 doors into your bakery.

That many more chances that a reader can discover your Magic Bakery and come in and sample more.

Take those 30 stories I wrote in April of 2017. I created 30 magic pies. Let's count the doors into my Magic Bakery I got from that month of having fun writing short fiction.

Each story will be published stand-alone. 30 x 12 = 360 doors.

Each will be put into a *Smith's Monthly* volume. About 8 volumes. 8 x 12 = 96 doors.

Each will be put in a five-story collection at some point. 6 collections. 6 x 12 = 72 doors.

So from writing 30 stories in 30 days and getting them out wide and in various forms, I created about 528 new entrance doors into my Magic Bakery. And who knows what the future of those 30 stories holds for even more doors.

That's why productivity is king in this new world. The more magic pies, the more doors into your bakery.

Now for Some Real Magic

The magic pie (your story) never leaves your bakery. Yet at the same time, that story exists out in all those places for readers to sample and find the door back to where that magic pie lives and all your other work lives.

Through the magic of copyright, your magic pie can be on the shelf in your store, completely in your control, while also being available for someone to license and read in electronic form all over the world.

So that is pretty nifty magic all by itself. It is the basis for the modern Magic Bakery.

But there is more. **The magic of paper copies.**

A paper copy of your book gets printed and sold. One reader found the door to your work. All great.

But that paper copy, **not the place it was sold**, but the paper copy itself, remains a door to your store as well.

How is that?

Say the book was read and then was donated to a library and sold there. So now that paper copy opened the door to your bakery for another reader.

This can't happen with electronic licenses. One sale, one customer. But not paper.

Say the book ends up in a used bookstore, the most magical place of all for opening doors to writer's Magic Bakeries. And someone finds it, takes it home, likes it and opens a door into your bakery.

Then trades the book back in or gives it to a library or to a friend.

So you have your work for sale on Amazon and a few other places in paper. Each place is a door to your bakery times the number of books you have in print.

But watch the number of sales each month in print, because each sale is a potential new door into your work for a reader or numbers of new readers at some point.

This concept has always been around, just never talked much about in the old traditional days. Writers back then only had one door and that was to sell the story to a publisher. And Magic Bakeries are pretty much non-existent when you sell all rights to traditional publishers.

But now paper copies can be a massive tool in bringing in loyal customers to your Magic Bakery because every paper book sold becomes a possible number of future doors.

The New World of Discoverability (I mean doors)

The thinking is simple: The more product you have in your Magic Bakery, the more possible doors there are out there for someone to find your work.

But you can see why I have always shouted about the silliness of being exclusive anywhere. It limits your doors into your bakery. It really is that simple.

And the more doors you have, the more people can find your Magic Bakery with all your work sitting gleaming on the shelves.

And the more product in your place, the more doors and the more readers will shop around when they do find you.

So above I said I have about 3,600 doors plus into my bakery. That number was based on just electronic license.

But hundreds of my books are in print and selling and each time one books sells, I know for a fact that one copy that sold might be a future door to a brand new customer.

And that's why sometimes my Magic Bakery gets real crowded with customers. And for any shop owner, that is a fun thing to see.

9

Success and the Future

Now there are two words that almost every writer I have met can't fathom or even see when it comes to their own writing and business.

Now granted, some writers give those two words lip service, and in different workshops Kris and I work at getting writers to think ahead. It feels like walking into a brick wall.

Success and future planning when it comes to writing and a publishing business are just not possible for almost every writer to fathom.

And honestly, I understand that. My goal, for a very long time, was to make a living at my writing. I had NO concept what that meant other than the basics of "paying my bills" with my writing income that month.

Notice the thought is making a living, not a career. A living can happen for a year. And a ton of writers in this modern world of indie publishing can make a living for a year or two, as long as the hot-new-trend they stumbled into continues.

You see this a great deal in the writers in Kindle Select. (And three years from the time I write this writers will be asking me "What was Kindle Select?") This book of blog posts will far, far outlast that blip in the publishing history.

These writers give no thought at all to building a career.

Let me give a quick definition that I use. "Making a Living" is a very short-term goal. "Building a Career" is the ability to make a living every year, year-after-year, over decades.

Everything I teach and everything in this book is aimed at helping writers build careers. If you want the most recent fad, go have fun. Bank the money is my suggestion.

So now, for this chapter, I am going to talk mostly about success.

Selling to Traditional Publishing

Got to deal with this first because to many beginning writers, simply selling to a major publisher is a success.

The sad writers who do this in 2017 (as I write this) are not giving one thought to the future or long-term career building. They are selling all rights to their books for a few thousand dollars and the pat on their heads that tells them that some English major in an office in New York really likes them.

Then for a short time a year or two later their books will be published overpriced, restricted in distribution, and with a great sense of "Is that all there is?"

Soon the book will be pushed to the back and forgotten, just an IP valuation on a corporate balance sheet. But wow is their family proud of them, but wonder why they are still working their day jobs.

To these writers success is measured by a sale to a single editor. That's it.

That's their definition of success. Sort of sad, huh?

And by signing the contract they make their future with those books very simple. They no longer own the books, so those books have no future.

⤳ Reality of Numbers

Publishing is a very large industry. Very large. And if you know how to manage your magic pies correctly, your work in publishing can extend into many other areas as well. Movies, television, games, to name just some obvious ones.

But writers tend to be focused on how to make an extra sale here, or give something away there, to gain more imaginary numbers on a mailing list. These writers make no plans and have no concept at all of what might happen when it comes to real success and real money.

One question we do in both the online monthly business class and a variation of it in the Strengths Business workshop, is what would happen if you knew suddenly that in three months 100,000 dollars would hit your account.

The answers are head-shaking because it is clear no writer we have asked that question to has thought ahead to that kind of small success. (And yes, that is a small success in publishing.)

And if you are thinking you would take that small success, I sure understand. But that also illustrates the problem. Your vision, your ability to see a future and real success, is very limited.

A good attorney friend of mine once said that he envied me with my job. He went to work, made great money, and then went home. All the money he could make in a day he made. To keep making money he had to go back to work the next day. But when I got up and went to writing, every day I had a chance of hitting a home run and making millions.

And sometimes that possibility was with a novel I wrote years before.

He saw the publishing profession so much better than most writers.

Sadly, there is nothing I can say to most here in this chapter to convince most anyone. Think about it. Even those who do make the huge money are always called "lucky" or "outliers" by those who can't imagine doing it themselves.

There is a vested interest in writers as a class to not think about real success or the future.

So What Do You Do to Get Ready for Success?

First, never sell your entire magic pie. For any reason to anyone.

Keep that magic pie, that copyright, firmly planted in your bakery.

That is the basic center of everything. Then your pie, as the future unfolds, can earn you money.

What else can you do?

—**Start studying writers who are successful in careers.** Not those flash writers chasing the most recent trend. Study writers who have been writing and selling and in a career in one form or another for decades. There are a lot of us.

—**Start understanding business and money.** Your Magic Bakery is a business. Start understanding things like cash streams, corporations, tax protections, and so on. For example, that 100,000 you get in suddenly. If you understand what I just said, you will keep it all. If you don't, you will pay over half of it to governments.

#4 —**Start learning how stories and novels get outside of publishing.** What do you need to do? Learn that.

#5 —**Get your work into every market you can around the world and let it build.** And keep writing what you love.

#6 —**Learn all the ways you can divide up your magic pies.**

#7 —**Then be patient.** You can't learn any of the above overnight, or even in a year.

You are a writer. Write the next book, the next story, the next blog post as I am doing here.

Then, as I am doing here, after you are finished, see how many ways you can turn slices of the pie you just created into cash streams.

Next chapter will be about thinking about the future. You know, that place beyond Christmas.

10

Beyond Next Year

As I said last chapter, it has been my observation that most writers never look more than a year out, if that. And that lack of being able to see five years and ten years and fifty years into the future causes all sorts of really bad decisions.

Now, I wish I could say I had been an exception to this in my first few decades or so in publishing. Nope. Kris was a bunch better at looking long term and making decisions based on that vision. But I wasn't. And wow did I make some bone-headed mistakes because of that lack of vision.

So now here I am trying to maybe help one or two people expand into the future their plans and hopes and focus.

The Magic Bakery

It is the future that really is important in a Magic Bakery. Let me try to explain why in just a couple simple points.

—Your copyright, your magic pie, will last and stay fresh for 70 years past your death (In the US, 50 years in other countries). At that 70 year mark your heirs will lose control over it, but that does not mean they still can't make money from it for another 70 years or longer.

—You have no idea what technology will be coming in the next century. No clue. (New ways to cut your magic pie.)

(Example: I wrote one of the very first electronic books Pocket Books ever published. The year was 2000 and trust me, even with electronic books being sort of in existence for a decade or more before that, I thought it stupid. Shows what I knew. Again, in those years I wasn't the best at seeing the future.)

—If you structure the business of your bakery correctly (a coming chapter), your business will not only make you a lot of money in your lifetime, but also survive you and thrive. But the business has to be set up for the future.

So Many Ways to Fail

Those three points above seem very simple and obvious, don't they? But wow can you fail in so many ways when you stand in your Magic Bakery, surrounded by all your magic pies, and have no sense of tomorrow.

Let me give you three major failure points.

—Sell your book to a major traditional publisher (or movie producer) for all rights for the term of the copyright. Pie vanishes from your bakery. Writers who do this give zero thought to the future of their business at all. To them their book has no value beyond the tiny pat on the head traditional publishers give them and a little bit of money. Or hope for a movie that won't get made.

—You don't learn business and sales, so your store sits there with few customers and eventually you drift away to do something else. Your pies never mold or grow old, but dust covers the shelves and paint peels off the front of your store and no one goes in. (This happens to 80-90% of all fiction writers, sadly.)

You all know this kind of thing. Your store becomes a "whatever-happened-to?" store. We have all walked down a mall, seen an empty spot and asked "Whatever happened to that place?" Imagine that was where your Magic Bakery was at and you get the sad idea of what happens when you quit.

—You don't understand how Intellectual Property (IP) works, so you make no preparation for the day something happens to you. So those 70 years plus that your Magic Bakery could remain open and flourishing and making your family or some charity money vanish when they dump your body in the ground.

All three of those major failure points are from lack of being able to deal with the future.

A Ticking Time Bomb

Remember a few chapters back I mentioned the new world of IP Valuation? Not your issue, right? Your stories only make a few hundred so they can't be worth much. Right?

Again, no thought to any future. Courts and estate probate judges are understanding IP valuation and are starting to apply different forms of evaluation. If you are making a nice bit of money from your stories and you have not set up the right structure to move your IP to your heirs, they could get hit with a tax bill upon your death that could destroy everything. Wouldn't that be a nice gift to leave your family?

Easily fixed if you think about the future at all. But alas, most writers don't.

And that leads to the next problem–

What Is Your Magic Bakery Worth?

Most newer writers and all traditionally published writers would say nothing. And the reason for that is that there are no pies on the shelves. The bakery is mostly empty.

Even if there were magic pies on those shelves, most writers would still say it wasn't worth much at all. Why? Because they can't see past a year or so.

Now I understand that moving forward, IP needs freshening at times to remain attractive to the current buyer. Not going to talk about that ongoing task. I know it all too well. So for this, I will assume you do that work, or have it done, or your estate will do it.

So if you can imagine that as a possibility, what might your bakery be worth?

For what amount would I sell all rights to all 300 of my magic pies, plus the bakery itself? What kind of future income do my 300 plus magic pies have possible?

And in three years that number will be past 400, and so on, not counting all the IP that will return to me under the 35 year rule starting in 2026.

Impossible to calculate. But fun to look at when you realize you really are creating something of value, even though it only sells five copies a year. It still has value.

Heinlein's Rule #2 states simply: Finish what you write.

When you finish a story, you have added value to your Magic Bakery. It really is that simple.

How to Learn to Think Forward

Sure, work to make money now. Work to sell your stuff now. But all the while, keep these basic things in mind.

—**Never allow your IP to leave your bakery.** You license slices, nothing more. For only the term needed and when the term is up that slice will magically appear back in your pie.

—**When discouraged, thinking of shutting the doors for good, do an inventory of your existing IP.** Then try to put a value on it, keeping in mind your lifetime and 70 years beyond. Imagine two or three things being made into movies, imagine others being games, still others being part of some unknown tech. Then write the next story or book and add even more value.

—**Learn Business.** Tons of great books for small businesses out there. Understand what a good year of growth might be. That will help with perspective instead of always listening to the latest fad from the latest hot guru of marketing and thinking you are not doing enough.

—**Learn Estates.** It will help you if you figure out a way to help your favorite family and/or charity with your business if you can get it large enough. In other words, write your fun stories for a larger purpose in the future.

—**Make It a Challenge.** You want to have the best bakery. The most successful. The larger, the nicer your bakery is, the more customers you will get, the more sales, the more value. But building the best bakery takes time. Growing any business takes time. Make it a challenge. Not something to be afraid of, but something to have fun with.

Summary

A wonderful thing about our Magic Bakeries: They really are magical.

Copyright is an amazing ingredient in our pies that allows us to build and run these wonderful places full of diverse products. And magically attract customers from all over the world.

Our magic pies can be enjoyed as a book, a movie, an audio file, in tons of different languages, and who knows what else is coming in the future. All without ever leaving our bakery.

Copyright also allows us the time to build these magical places.

You just have to know that the future is out there and first accept it, then plan for it.

11

Maintenance

This book, at its heart, has been about the business of fiction. And selling fiction. And the copyright associated with fiction.

Fact: So many writers ignore copyright and eventually go away. Long-term writers know copyright and know how to get every bit of money we can from copyright. That might be the most important element to why a long-term writer is a long-term writer and not a "what-ever-happened-to" writer.

Fact: So many writers equate the hours it took to write something with the value of the story. A short story can't have much value because it only took four hours to write it. That is the thinking. I hear that all the time with writers afraid to charge a fair value for their short stories. Head-shaking.

And those two "facts" cause extreme problems, both large and small. And where those two facts come into play the most is in the long-term maintenance of copyright.

How I Learned Value

Early on as a writer, I too equated the value of the time spent with the value of the story. Now understand, I considered myself expensive. I would never sell a story for under 5 cents per word and almost never did a media book for less than $20,000. Often a lot more and ghost novels even more than that.

And I could spend hours writing every day, so I was considered fast. And thus it didn't take me much time at all to earn that advance on a novel or the sale money from a short story. So in my head I had set some value for my work at the amount I could get out of it and that was related to the time I spent writing it.

One simple story fairly early in my career quickly proved to me how stupid that very short-sighted thinking was. The story was called "In the Shade of the Slowboat Man." I wrote it in under three hours while sitting facing Nina Kiriki Hoffman in a living room at a writer's retreat. It was one of three short stories I did in that day or so.

It was for a vampire anthology, but the editor bounced it because it was too "nice" for his anthology. So I was about to toss it in a drawer when Kris forced me to send it to Ed Ferman at F&SF and he bought it. And then it was on the final Nebula ballot that year and in the Nebula Awards Anthology as well. Cool. I made a little more than I expected from it. But my worldview as to value and time was still intact.

Until I got an offer for a radio play for the short story and they hired Kris to write the script. And suddenly that three-hour short story made us another $10,000 and was turned into a really great radio play.

And then the story got picked up for a number of reprint

places and optioned once for a movie and I made money on all that. (I still think it would make a great movie.)

And then I ended up reprinting it in Smith's Monthly and also putting it up as a stand-alone for $2.99 in electronic and $4.99 in paper and it sells regularly every year for years now.

Three hours. One simple short story. Twenty-plus years after I wrote the short story, it is still earning me money, more money every year than I expected to get from it at first.

That was the first story that finally got me realizing the long-term value of copyright. I have other short stories now that I have made more money on. "Jukebox Gifts" as an example.

Those magic pies are very popular with the customers of my Magic Bakery.

Maintenance of the Magic Bakery

As I said last chapter, magic pies do not spoil.

But sadly, they can be forgotten. And often are.

Now at the ten-year mark of indie publishing, there are statistics coming out now about the large percentage of stories and books that sell no copies in a year. (This was always the case before, but no one talked about that.)

Think of all the billions of stories and novels now available to readers as a giant ocean. In this new world, the stories that sell are the ones on the surface of the giant ocean of fiction available to readers.

The ones that don't sell are far, far below the surface, down in the dark, impossible to find or sell.

Now when I started into indie publishing, I had over a hundred published traditional novels, over 60 of which were under this name. And everyone thought that I was lucky. Used to make me very angry when someone would say that because I knew the truth. I wasn't lucky. I considered someone starting fresh lucky. I had a massive wall in front of me to climb over.

When you clicked on my name on Amazon back then, all you saw was Star Trek, Men in Black, gaming novels and so on. Books I had been paid for and didn't make another dime on and did not own the magic Pie.

So when I started I put up in fairly quick order over 50 of my own short stories. When you clicked on Amazon, my highest short story was nine pages deep in the list of 50 plus pages of my novels and stories at that point.

Deep is the operative word there. My stories were way, way deep under the surface and impossible to see. Driven to the depths by my success in traditional publishing.

So I knew I only had one choice if I was going to make a career under this name in this modern world. I had to churn the surface of the ocean of books and do a lot of product and basically overwhelm the system. And I did. Not with any promotion tricks, but with simple production.

And it took me years.

Do those early stories I put up now sell? Very few of them, because I haven't spent the time and energy to bring them back to the surface. (I will. All planned, actually.)

They are magic pies, sitting on my shelves in my bakery, but I have turned the lights off on that corner of the bakery. No one can see the pies, so they don't buy any of them.

So maintenance of the inventory of the bakery is critical. And difficult.

A Sample of Maintenance

Kris has figured out a way to keep the older stories and

novels from sitting in a corner with the lights off. For the short stories, she puts up a free short story on her blog every week. She has been doing this for years and years.

The story is still for sale on all the wide markets, of course. Only free on her blog.

And when she puts the story up for free, often WMG puts a new cover on it if it is an older story, we redo the blurb, and so on. In other words, she brushes off the dust from the magic pie and puts a spotlight over the pie and makes it a weekly special in her bakery.

And the story not only is free, but people buy it that week and often the story will keep on selling at a decent pace for some time to come.

Value for Decades

Magic pies can last a very long time if you are smart with contracts and don't let the entire pie leave your bakery. The pies can last for at least 50 or 70 years past your death (depending on your country) and even after that they will still have value.

But they will not have much value if you do not maintain them.

Magic Bakeries are like any other retail store. The inventory must be kept clean, the lights on for customers to see the product, and the door unlocked for anyone to enter from anywhere in the world.

There must also be someone to run the business and keep the bills paid, even after you die.

But more than anything else, the inventory must be moved around at times, displays changed, standard sales techniques used.

And the value of each pie in your bakery can't be determined by either the year you created the pie or the time it took to create. Your customers will not care about any of that.

You, the owner of the Magic Bakery must believe in every pie. And if the lights over a pie start to flicker, change the bulb.

Summary

I'm surprised, but the Magic Bakery, as a metaphor for copyright and the fiction writing business, does not seem to stretch too far in any area. When I started this, I thought it would.

Some basics I hope you got from this book in one metaphor or another.

—Writers need to learn to think like real businesses.

—Writers need to learn to think like retail and wholesale businesses.

—Writers need to learn copyright so they understand the ingredients of each pie they are creating and how the magic works.

—And writers, lastly, need to give value to their own work. Both as it is created, the year after it was created, and a hundred years after it was created.

The ocean full of reading will not be decreasing. So it is up to each writer to keep their stories near the surface and readers and buyers coming into their Magic Bakeries.

Now this book, this magic pie will take its rightful place in my bakery. I hope you enjoyed it as much as I did writing it.

And if you did, I hope you will try another pie. After all, magic pies are not fattening.

EPILOGUE

A Comment Reminded Me of Something

As I said, I did this book in a series of blogs on my website. And there were some great comments along the way. One brought up this last short chapter.

I used to wonder what rights I could sell to my fiction. What exactly those rights were all called. I thought for the longest time there were rules and I just couldn't find the rules or the secret door to go through to discover where those rules were posted.

I think all of us feel that way early on because we don't understand the true nature of copyright when we start writing. In fact, most writers, even though they will spend years writing, don't have a clue what they are trying to sell or license. And won't spend one minute trying to learn it.

Let alone learn the real nature of copyright, the deep down nature of it. That takes time to really understand.

So the truth? There is no magic list of what you can and

can't sell in your copyright. Or what the names are of those magical things you slice out of your copyright pie.

And there are certainly no rules.

NONE.

ZERO. ZIP. ZILCH.

It took me some time to realize that as well.

I wanted to know what exactly First Serial Rights meant and First Anthology Rights, or Non-exclusive Anthology Rights and so on and so on, not realizing those are just made-up terms for contracts to help two parties define exactly what is needed.

And the reason those terms are used regularly, if you actually look at the terms, is because they clearly define a way to slice a copyright pie.

In essence, what I am trying to say is this: To describe the piece of your copyright pie you are licensing to another person in a contract, **you can call it anything the two of you agree to that will be clear as to what is being licensed.**

Now I had a comment wishing I had put more "meat" in my *Magic Bakery* book. The person had hoped I would define all that stuff. Even if I had tried, I would be wrong for the very next contract you saw.

How can I define terms, put meat, as the comment said, in an article when the very question shows a lack of knowledge of copyright in contracts?

There is no meat past you learning copyright and understanding that you are free to define the slice of your pie in any way you see fit. **As long as you and the person on the other side of the contract agree to the definition or name you put on it.**

The Magic Bakery was an attempt at helping with some basic understanding of copyright and business in this new world of publishing. I put all the "meat" I could in it and still keep it at a basic level.

As a young writer, not understanding copyright, I would have been disappointed as well that the book didn't give the secret handshake and the location of where all those terms were hidden.

Ahh, well. I knew the danger of trying to do a book on copyright in a world where writers are flat determined to not learn it.

So let me start the list of "meat" for those of you still looking for the sacred scroll of terms locked in that hidden vault in a Chicago basement. Then maybe you will understand the vault really is empty.

Example: Take your most recent magic pie off the shelf and get out a sharp magic knife. Then cut out a very, very thin slice to license and in the contract for that slice you can call that license "First North American Refrigerator Magnet Rights."

You can and should reserve "First English Refrigerator Magnet Rights" in the contract because you never know about those companies in other parts of the world. (A different slice.)

Also hold back all "Refrigerator Magnet Translation Rights." (Yet another slice.)

And make sure you are clear in your terms in your contract that the right does not include "First North American Button Rights." (Yet another slice.)

And make sure you say that all other rights are reserved to the author so nothing leaves your magic pie by accident.

Those are all real rights, folks, and if you can't figure out what they are, just slowly say aloud the name of the slice. The words describe the slice of the pie you are licensing.

It really is that simple.

As I said numbers of times in different chapters, every pie can be sliced into thousands of slices, limited only by your imagination on how to limit a right and your understanding of the basic nature of copyright.

As one reader said, and gave me permission to repeat, there is a simple formula for all of this.

The DJ Formula...

Time position + territory + language + usage = rights

Time Position = First, Second, Third, etc.

Territory = hemisphere, country, state, moon, Mars, etc.

Language = English, French, Spanish, etc.

Usage = anything that displays text, images, such as radio, movies, books, plays, comics, buttons, tea towels, etc.

Use that formula anytime you are trying to figure out how to slice your magic pie. It will do wonders to help you through any confusion you might have.

Hope that helps some with adding "meat" into the book. Magic Meat I suppose.

And finally, the metaphor stretched too far and broke.

70

Be the first to know!

Just sign up for the Dean Wesley Smith newsletter, and keep up with the latest news, releases and so much more—even the occasional giveaway.

So, what are you waiting for? Sign up at deanwesleysmith.com.

But wait! There's more. Sign up for the WMG Publishing newsletter, too, and get the latest news and releases from all of the WMG authors and lines, including Kristine Kathryn Rusch, Kristine Grayson, Kris Nelscott, *Fiction River: An Original Anthology Magazine, Smith's Monthly,* and so much more.

With more than a hundred published novels and more than seventeen million copies of his books in print, *USA Today* bestselling author Dean Wesley Smith follows five simple business rules for writing fiction. And now, he shares how those rules helped shape his successful career.

In this WMG Writer's Guide, Dean takes you step-by-step through Heinlein's Rules and shows how following those rules can change your writing—and career—for the better.

Simple rules, yet deceptively hard to follow. Do you have the courage to take a hard look at your writing process and follow Heinlein's Rules? Dean shows you how.

"Dean Wesley Smith's blog gives both a slightly different view of the publishing world than I'd seen before and detailed hands-on "here's how to get from A to B" instruction."
—Erin M. Hartshorn, *Vision: A Resource for Writers*

ABOUT THE AUTHOR

Considered one of the most prolific writers working in modern fiction, *USA Today* bestselling writer Dean Wesley Smith published far more than a hundred novels in forty years, and hundreds of short stories across many genres.

At the moment he produces novels in several major series, including the time travel Thunder Mountain novels set in the Old West, the galaxy-spanning Seeders Universe series, the urban fantasy Ghost of a Chance series, a superhero series starring Poker Boy, and a mystery series featuring the retired detectives of the Cold Poker Gang.

His monthly magazine, *Smith's Monthly*, which consists of only his own fiction, premiered in October 2013 and offers readers more than 70,000 words per issue, including a new and original novel every month.

During his career, Dean also wrote a couple dozen *Star Trek* novels, the only two original *Men in Black* novels, Spider-Man and X-Men novels, plus novels set in gaming and television worlds. Writing with his wife Kristine Kathryn Rusch under the name Kathryn Wesley, he wrote the novel for the NBC miniseries The Tenth Kingdom and other books for *Hallmark Hall of Fame* movies.

He wrote novels under dozens of pen names in the worlds

of comic books and movies, including novelizations of almost a dozen films, from *The Final Fantasy* to *Steel* to *Rundown*.

Dean also worked as a fiction editor off and on, starting at Pulphouse Publishing, then at *VB Tech Journal*, then Pocket Books, and now at WMG Publishing, where he and Kristine Kathryn Rusch serve as series editors for the acclaimed *Fiction River* anthology series.

For more information about Dean's books and ongoing projects, please visit his website at www.deanwesleysmith.com and sign up for his newsletter.

For more information:
www.deanwesleysmith.com

Made in the USA
Columbia, SC
05 August 2017